EATING THE ARCHIVE

Born and educated in Baddawi refugee camp, **Yousif M. Qasmiyeh** is a poet and translator whose doctoral research at the University of Oxford examines containment and the archive in 'refugee writing'. Time, the body, and ruination inform his poetry and prose, which have appeared in journals including *Modern Poetry in Translation, Stand, Critical Quarterly, GeoHumanities, Cambridge Literary Review, PN Review, Poetry London* and *New England Review*. Yousif is the Creative Encounters Editor of the *Migration and Society* journal, and his collection, *Writing the Camp* (Broken Sleep Books, 2021) was a Poetry Book Society Recommendation, and was shortlisted for the Royal Society of Literature's Ondaatje Prize.

Also by Yousif M. Qasmiyeh

Writing the Camp (Broken Sleep Books, 2021)

In *Eating the Archive*, Yousif M. Qasmiyeh offers object lessons on what is — and isn't — graspable: a photograph, a frying pan, a gun, language, time, prayer, a mirror, a razor, a divination bowl. Who is the author of the archive? The poet bears witness, to what lives and dies right in front of him, and inside him. He does this by writing, 'a trace still as it is still.' To read Yousif M. Qasmiyeh is to step into a caesura: a place where presence and absence engage with attention; a place where erasure speaks back; a camp of voices that refuse to be forgotten or silent.

— Pádraig Ó Tuama, *Poetry Unbound*

Federico Garcia Lorca suggested that every poet has a wound, but what if, as Yousif M. Qasmiyeh writes in his new book *Eating the Archive*, 'the wound is continuously postponed'? Enter memory lodged with shrapnel, where to view anything culminates in breathing through time that 'cuts through words'. This vast and beautifully parablesque second collection by Qasmiyeh is a poetics of rupture, of cracks and fissures. Here we find a writer so philosophically alert to the crossing of danger that is 'experience'. With a knack for echolalic narrative, Qasmiyeh is able to both fragment and distil time, looping back to remember and re-remember what happened to the author and his family from their time in Lebanon's Baddawi refugee camp. *Eating the Archive* offers us a densely physical consideration of language—the difficulties of writing to name anything that comes from the archive of mind and body through to the 'limb of a word'—where writing itself is risk. Qasmiyeh is one of the most exciting new writers of the twenty-first century.

— James Byrne, *Of Breaking Glass*

Qasmiyeh's camp is a space for reckoning. In his poems, home is a tomb and the present is situated in the afterlife of history, as he calls it, where there is "No one to question our dying. No one to shed a tear for what is happening behind walls. Thin, flawed walls built for the temporary in mind." The field some have begun to call the literature of displacement is where the world's most important writing is taking place and Qasmiyeh's second collection confirms that he is one of its brightest rising talents.

— André Naffis-Sahely, *The Promised Land: Poems from Itinerant Life*

Eating The Archive by Yousif M. Qasmiyeh is a poetic counter-archive of the refugee camp. It visibilises what is otherwise rendered invisible in the official archives. Qasmiyeh's poems "can see," emerging powerfully from prolonged waiting in the camp, where "waiting is seeing". This important book is an invitation to think in the cracks of the walls, where cracks and the spaces of in-betweenness are also witnesses for wounded names and faces – a space where the poet can breathe in his mother tongue by breathing with his mother. *Eating The Archive* is an open gateway to encounter the camp that is lost in conventional ethnographic observations and fieldwork.

— Shahram Khosravi, *'Illegal' Traveller*

© 2023 Yousif M. Qasmiyeh. All rights reserved; no part of this book may be reproduced by any means without the publisher's permission.

ISBN: 978-1-915079-67-1

The author has asserted their right to be identified as the author of this Work in accordance with the Copyright, Designs and Patents Act 1988

Cover designed by Aaron Kent

Edited and typeset by Aaron Kent

Broken Sleep Books Ltd
Rhydwen,
Talgarreg,
SA44 4HB
Wales

Contents

Time is a Swelling	13
The Table	16
UNRWA	18
For the Coming Silence	23
The Hair	25
Writing With My Mother	26
Prayers	28
The Divination Bowl	29
Sacrifices	30
The Camp	31
The Edge	32
In Anticipation	34
The Camp is a Bait for Time	35
To Belong in Dust	39
Other Remains	40
A Poem	41
The Language of Hell	42
The Tree	43
A Photograph For My Mother's Absence	45
My Mother's Photograph or A Deferred Epitaph	48
The Crack Invites	50
The Wait	51
Suddenness	52
The Secret	53
Survival	54
The Heart is Tomorrow's Absence	55
Vows	56
english	57
Circumcision	60
The Bride	61

Offers	62
Communion	64
The War	67
Congruence	68
The Razor	69
The Trap	70
Dwelling	71
Holy Water	72
Ailments	73
On Living	75
Haram	76
The Name	80
A Gate Cut Out of Dreams	83
Wreathed in Vowels	87
For it is a Calf	88
English	90
The Body	91
Home is a Tomb	92
Letters of Ailment	95
The Story	96
To Wait is to See	100
Abolition	101
Slain Intentions	104
Ketchup! Ketchup!	107
Prayers II	108
The Ration Card	110
A Decent Burial	112
The Cull	113
Holes	114
Family Album	116
Acknowledgements	119

Eating the Archive

Yousif M. Qasmiyeh

For Kheizeran – in words and in silence

One remembers having been, but one does not remember having lasted.
— Gaston Bachelard, *Intuition of the Instant*

Time is a Swelling

The past, out of all times, is what can be seen in eyes long gone.

To see the past as a happening in its shade, my mother would carefully sift our UN-gifted grains: the dry for us and the hovering bits for birds that never were.

What we ate was what she planted in secret under her pillow: remains of nothing in the shape of distant prayers.

I was not alone.
My mother, with a cane and poor eyesight, was to my right
[Nothing to our left]

Now I hold her by the hand like a drifting sound
heart to heart, throat to throat
to walk together

Bodies hung in thin air
the sweat of old age and time
suspended returns to the eyes that once saw.

You say to the clock hung adjacent to all religious things in the room: *My time is a swelling, my mother's yeast for the aged bread left aside as proof for time.*

Nothingness, hide not in imagination. Nor ascend the psalms of night. What is left, for you and me, is the suspicion in suspicion.

When the sky is just a crow, with air raids as infinite as their ruins, the body's task is to ponder its body: here, in this place, people ascend to normality on crutches.

A body alone feasts on the body.

I shall imagine my tongue drowning in languages that are not mine so as to speak in water.

Seeing is the thing's substitute. What is deferred in seeing is the thing for its only time.

To pretend not to see what is amassing in your hands while you carry a heart barely attached to your body. To pretend all is well for once while they prod you in the back to remind you that it is time to look.

I ask – a question for me: *What it is in writing that has no such thing as a present but is written –*
solely written –, for a future subject to many pasts?

They would normally write their names in graphite so they would rub them out and write them again as names for suspected names.

I begged her to take me with her. Then, I could see what she could do to her eyes in wakes: tears in the aftermath of tears, her veil slowly unravelling, two loose ends caressing my grandmother's dead face.

What the eyes could see was not all. There were many. Some carrying what they could in haste: sponge mattresses, plastic bags stuffed with memories, children on backs and in slings … It was in the dead of night when almighty shrieks were heard. As recounted by my mother, it was my father who first ran to find out. When he returned, sweat pouring down his face and elapsed body, he uttered no words. Instead, he pulled the bed sheet over his face to sob alone.

Whose eyes are forever stones?

Tombstones are witnesses to the never witnessed.

Tears are gifts to the blind.

The bird that lost its way into the camp was chased by screaming children until it was lost again.

The same bird was not announced dead. For it to become permissible to eat, it is to be slain in the future.

To this day, in the camp the word *origin* is used to allude to a distant tense.

In those distant and near origins, time pronounces its face in the absence of a body.

It is the camp that makes Palestine near. When I say the camp, I say what it is that is not the camp.

To become a camp is to come and become simultaneously.

In poetry, the wound is continuously postponed.

The Table

> *You've made a table you say, and are happy*
> — Tom Paulin

the nails are deep
in the flesh
different shapes and sizes
rusty heads
                             bent

recitations for a job well done
prayers
for wood elevated to the body

for the cross in the backyard

what he made for my mother
who spent her years giving birth
to eleven heads
one after the other

different shapes and sizes

from wooden slats
once an old window
shared with the neighbours

those hands hurt no soul
meeting through the net
clutching when darkness falls

UNRWA replacing the wood
but not the window

the holey net

he dismantled every whole to make fragments

then with an axe
splitting sounds into further sounds
rendering cracks into noise

uneven legs for a body
nails protruding

                              crucifixion

assembled
elevated
the feast that never was

UNRWA

for it is the home erected in absentia
retaining nothing in the name of forgetting
stomachs hounding sounds and stones
the inedible as the sufficient
the possibility that time is infinite
gratitude towards god
and others
god's time and timelessness
and whoever feigns tears
tears on us
pitying tears
on the grandparents
rushing out of time
the parents as heirs of journeys
the sisters
the brothers in uniform
with swords cleaner than Don Quixote's
with buttons   some loose   some absent
with looks for the blonde ethnographer
initials wreathed in a distant future
for those who no longer exist
or exist as dead
who live but not live
whose names are the same
not as their own names but as those of the disappearing
the ones coming when the body is no more
initials to repeat
initials to recite
the limb of a word
the limbs of words
words summoned afterwards

in the aftermath of fallen bodies
like tombstones engraved at last
for corpses
maimed like the letters
for texts
half-written, some stuck in throats
I say   *UNRWA*
the word as the throat

pronouncing the dead alive
they say

returning their words in our sounds
we say

till words are affinities
charms on the hollow guts
vows for the undetermined in life and living
a home as neat as non-existence
for the refugee
all for breathless memories
departure
of feet treading and treading on time
of cries near but distant
of reluctant mourning devoid of speech

what is gathered is for tomorrow
what is left behind is for all time
a thing or things for the then time
time as a bag
of plurals
no buttons to seal its ends
no stitching to call it a thing
only the bare as the bare

the rim   that invites
the rim   that pronounces

its rim

satiated with what is within grasp
sufficient for the moment
that time
memories and other things

time not to gather any crops
time not to lead the scattered beasts out of time
time is as it is
a photograph
photographs of faces
of a present in the past
of people like people
swaying to gasp
swaying to live without life

photographs of sorrow seeping through the air
like weightless ash
ashen faces
beings of stone
bodies becoming ruins in their presence
the humming of nature
in deserted fields
the abyss inside garments
feet in the front
feet enmeshed in bodies
like extinct souls
petrified beings running from sea to sea
there is no longer a place
but only a time
bereaved dialects

words going astray
where sounds are mere signs
gesturing at things
no knowledge to comprehend the thinness of air
nor is there a scale for tomorrow
what happens, happens
in their palms and inside them is the truth
of what remains

in time things come
they depart
with metaphors laden as clear as the sun
all they do is wait
they wait as they walk
senseless directions
cleansed horizons
no scene for the eye save its own

they eat in hindsight
things that belong to the earth
things from those of twisted tongues
gifted under the name
wrapped in shade

the hostile in the host
the conditional in all pronouncements
the hosted at arm's length
armless like old fields

what is given is for the mouth
in the eye's absence
eyes retreating to their holes
whole eyes

memory is green

what is given is not eternally given
for it to become a thing it relinquishes its hands
forever other
for him to become himself he rises from ash
from time
from all that is absence
from nothing

eat
eat the palpable of what is there
eat ravenously
to recognise senses as memories for the then
the smell of what will be
the taste as medicine

For the Coming Silence

I
Through the colander, water leaves and never leaves.

II
Face is a mere direction. Guide me, O face, to my face.

III
Rocking is noise sacrificed for the coming silence.

IV
Suddenly, I think of who I am to remember memory in memory.

V
In my hands is a prophecy. For I am a poet I follow in my footsteps to the hereafter.

VI
Sorrow is but the body replete with its own silence.

VII
The tree cut for fire is still burning in my heart.

VIII
Whether in speech or in sex, inside the mouth lies another mouth.

IX
Is not that wailing in language, the wailing of the body over its body?

X
Yousif,
the name I see in black,
The transliterated version of the name, almost as pronounced in life by the mother,
as archived by the strangers with slit tongues

The name that appears and disappears in equal measure
the one guarded, unarmed

XI
In wars, trembling makes the body and not the other way around.

XII
I say to fear: *Whatever you do, do it to no-one.*

The gun I cradled when my moustache was barely there was that of a dead person whose blood was still fresh on the strap.

For what it is, sense only loses itself in the tangible. What my father held then was the shrapnel protruding from his own flesh.

When the war started, fighter jets low and high, all gathered on the doorstep bearing a bundle of our things, staring back at the door, my father said: *Let's go and die in bed.*

He taught me how to peel an orange in one go – one long peel with two beginnings.

The Hair

My sister

I shall write the stitch on your veil.

Yours before mine –

a pact between us
a text we hide in *hair* and *poetry*

in multiply-darned letters
free of diacritics,

like our shared quilt.

Writing With My Mother

My mother
                        the rood so I hang in there
staring at my own falls

For all she knows
All she does not know.

We write together –

We co-write despite the tongue

For each other's sake

In the hope of seeing in lamenting
memories the shape of a cask

To them we set sight

To co-see

Because honing the kitchen knives is never a thing,

she awaits the lack as it is

Because the heart is born old, it hardly leaves her sight

The beats it now shepherds

The worries she hands to me with a trusted hand
nothing is normal
nothing is a constant tense

We scrub the sound with a *loofa* grown inside our house
    cut
   dried
  deseeded   across the neighbour's wall.

We scrub the skin –
What we call dead,
The cracks in history and in the flesh
to clasp that metal inside

She in voice
        Dialectal patterns

I with what I heired of words

                to convert the voice into religion

Prayers

It cannot be earth.
Nor can it be the loose threads in translation,
those of a dialect
uttered
so as to be gathered in pales
wide enough for suspended times.

The sinking forehead
in the overworn paths,
drowning
for the body
instead of the body.

The indented trace for the face that shall be.
The route to heaven.
The apparent route to all things.

What she waters,
day and night,
in total absence for a bare presence
that shall be recited through the palm.

The tentative texture,
interwoven,
never static,
where my mother's prostrating head once lay.

The Divination Bowl

Fear not a human.

With no recourse to what is next, they poured the water out of the bowl and waited for fear to return.

Despite it not being ours, we surround it with our dead to make it ours.

What they did was unheard of. A secret so it roams and never returns. When my grandmother was counting the days on her fingers, she was counting her breath as patience.

Patience is to wait with eyes open wide.

Give him water from the bowl! We called it the bowl of fear to pray for its disappearance in secret.

Despite having two, we would borrow our neighbour's.

To nail what is broken in life, my father would bite his finger to bleed for pain.

Everything is sacrificial. Sometimes I wonder if there will be anybody left to sacrifice.

And we shall say things again. Sometimes the way they are. Sometimes as spectres marauding their own shadows.

Suffice it to say that what we dream of happens only in the reality that we crave for, but never takes place beyond the remit of itself as a dream.

Sacrifices

For him, a sharp knife is akin to remembering what really matters in life: a recollection of what it is that sustains imagination as a sight of contradictions by the sheer power of friction.

My father would normally sharpen his with another. A relentless rubbing whose risk never outweighs the intended outcome, a constant reminder of how a minimal loss in metal is the shortest route to blood.

Metal rubbing against our raw ears as we listen in awe and pain, looking at each other's faces and nodding whenever nodding is needed. For him, it is more for protecting us from those in the vicinity and less for slaying beasts.

I was a small child then, seven or eight, when he caught me trying to sneak our kitchen knife into my school bag. He did not utter a word. With tears pouring behind his thick glasses, he placed the knife where it belonged, amidst other knives.

The Camp

If all that is written
is written for a reason
then there is no time
for the camp.

The Edge

I
To distance himself from the camp, my brother bought a house on the edge.

The edge is not just the far end of the camp but where the camp starts and ends.

He says: *Borrowed eyes are somebody else's, irrespective of the seen.*

II
The life of those who come to us from time to time is only a life lived outside.

I remember my father leaving his wet socks on the windowsill where no sun ever shines.

His intention was to wait for his socks to dry with time.

III
A shade of patience is to kill the bird when trapped.

However you turn. Whatever you shun with the intention of shunning the coming, you shun the thing that is called life.

The hair that grows on the edge of my face and to you is clearly the seen that returns to me is for me the text that is to be rubbed off and rewritten with the least collateral damage.

IV

Using it to allude to something that is still ambiguous is in no way a lessening of ambiguity. The ambiguous flies away as one and never in flocks.

Close your eyes to see the ambiguous as the body.

The formations announced by the children's squeals will continue their journey mutely.

V

Repentance! Repentance for the things that shall remain unblurred to be forgiven.

In Anticipation

What we did, my brother and I, was clean outside our house and sprinkle water on the walls in anticipation of those walking past us with an open camera.

What they photograph is not us but a version of those who wish to be left alone and for whatever reason can no longer speak.

A photograph alone can counter existential surplus.

Under our breath: *Archiving our life begins with parting company with the stones in our lentils.*

The Camp is a Bait for Time

With the shovel, my father reclaims the echo. Blow after blow until the wheat wakes …
The camp preserves its metaphors in the same way it shields its navel from the seen.
Navel: a scar to itself.
There, in the time that remains, camps raise their bodies as they raise their absence.
If it alludes to anything, it alludes to the inheritance of water.

Like her mother, my mother scythes dryness in her dreams.
When my grandmother left her village, she died for her mother.
My mother's question: *Is dying, in the camp, history?*
To see the camp is to see its metonymies.
Only once his olive tree died, did my grandfather make himself a walking stick.
The proper noun, that is, what names, names nothing except the name.

The Camp is a Bait for Time.

Who testifies for who in the camp?
To testify is to occupy time verbally.
A custodian to itself it is: when survival is pondered by those in the camp, it is necessarily pondered in the future.
The camp: a covenant between Man and time.
When time is killed, time alone can testify to its killing.
Where is the mouth apropos the testimony?
Can it be that mourning is the camp?

The Camp is a Bait for Time.

Between consciousness and its face, and with a stick as erect as his old back, he would say: *Leave me to it. Leave me to its time.*

I write the camp as it is suspended in the written. In the actual written it is not. Nor is it in the absolute literality that suspiciously grasps the written.

I say: *Writing, like grasping, germinates the absent.*

What I write, I write for the disappearing hand, for the senility above, for what was a season, or a lapse, for its looming return to life in its form, deformed.

I write to testify to my hand, to the limb in me, above all else.

The suspected fears of the absent.

For those who live at the pace of time, within the means of a dialect. A dialect that will come late to their dry throats because of a looming air raid or the imminent death of a passer-by.

The thoughts that may wait to be picked off their well-bathed, dry bodies.

This is living, living as life in the future, as suspected time.

The Camp is a Bait for Time.

I am not sure if there is one Baddawi. Nor am I sure if there is life. The camp is also guilty of the name.

For it is a secret at birth: it is a camp.

In the camp, a tense for the inactive in the air is benevolently called the future.

Is it complicity between time and its offspring or is it the camp left to its own time?

In traces, the subject fights with the subject.

For a trace to endure as a trace, a dissolution of all things must ensue.

Could writing be a trace?

What follows mourning is mourning to the extent that neither the mourned nor the mourner know who is who.

The gravedigger digs to bury and digs to see.
Seeing is a cradle to the unseen.
To dig is to justify digging with or without a reason.
He always digs from the edges. He says: *Dig not the inside! The edges eat into the inside until no inside remains.*
When dug, a hole is no longer a hole. Sublimated, revered and stuffed with its own innards, it becomes a shrine.
In death, masks spit out their faces.
Rocked by the oncoming feet they die until another time.
Cemeteries in the camp are a discreet acknowledgment of that which is to come, in the sense that he who dies is he who survives time.

The Camp is a Bait for Time.

In the first person I see the camp.
[The camp to my eyes. My eyes to the camp.]
A camp it will be, the indefinite in the definite, a covenant for the place, for time promised as anniversaries.
At every anniversary, my father remembers his face and forgets my mother's.
What my father remembers can and cannot be his face.
To this day, he reminds me that I fell off his back.
In his presence, I await myself to say what must be said.
Neither he nor I remember whose language it is we speak.

Dying substantiates dying. Straying while dying always grants the gravedigger more time to widen his imagination.

Blame not a hand not knowing its hand.
In the camp, people die out of their time. Claiming the opposite, pronounce the camp a place.
This is not to say that the camp is other or unique as other: what is said is wholly said for the ruins before and after the place.
In principle, the unique lies outside life.

Those who cannot see their limbs have not yet been born.
In my language, only the static is granted the right of birth and a father.
Even though waiting is premised on seeing, their eyes never meet.
We wait with no eyes.
Can the blurriness in a child's eye be the sacred?
The sacred is nothing but absence.
The forbiddance of narration, the forbiddance of quenching one's thirst.

I remember with all my might.
I remember, hands anticipating my fall.
I remember, drenched in guilt, marching back to the disaster, to the details of the dead, with strict chronologies and smells.
I remember so I am alone, digging. Digging in the camp with my father's shovel.
I remember my mother ripping out her hair in anticipation of the future.
I remember my hand stealing my mother from my sisters in broad daylight.

The Camp is a Bait for Time.

To Belong in Dust

Where they dig will one day be a place
for him to rest
for some thing to be called a thing
to belong in dust

For a body to sprout in absence
to render and
be rendered a time

Whispers for the living
Whispers for the dead

They dig
arms stretching beyond
overstretching
clanking shovels

Casting the abundance of mud
to the side
weary faces
sweat perching on tears

Other Remains

From his mouth to ours
that was before he quit smoking
halves of pears
apples   punctured in the middle with might
Anything,
Everything

Further halved under his ageing teeth
Tobacco-tinged
Saliva
His saliva,
Other remains
Lurking in our mouths

A Poem

I dream of writing a poem that can see.
One whose eyes are crystalline.
Whose arms are of multitudinous fire.

Words rubbing, overhearing their departure.
Their return.
Clenched fists, remedies ground for life, tales to tell.

A poem for the end.

The Language of Hell

carries the ultimate fire in its old heels, snapping at disappearance
the moment it is uttered

can imitate the dead with and without their bodies

has the colour of redness, but is not red

groans whenever we descend into uncertain hope

holds you by the throat if you dare not fear

has the wail of a widower

The Tree

It is rare to see trees in the camp. I remember seeing or hearing my father saying that we once had a pomegranate tree in our house but because we needed space to accommodate yet another arrival he got rid of it. We all agreed it was a wise decision.

The tree is gone but my father never built on its stump.

"My mother is nowhere to be seen. Nowhere to be captured entirely."

A Photograph For My Mother's Absence

Out of a tin box full of needles, of different sizes and shapes, with wonky and straight eyes, alongside loose and rolled-up threads of subdued colours, I picked it up. Without even looking in her hardly-open eyes to seek consent, I snatched it, to see it at close range and in the company of my tears: a photograph of my mother's face wandering alone in her ever-shrinking pastures. At first I put it in my pocket, then moved it to my wallet alongside my identity card for Palestinian refugees and the draft of a love letter I once wrote for my brother to his lover in graphite and traces of ink to give the impression of age. The letter reached the lover but my ID and my mother's picture are still in one another's company.

An eye for an eye so both my mother and I could see in each other's eye what it is to be seen: dissipating edges; black and white losing their blackness and whiteness for the sake of a third tinge; speckled surfaces; eyes looking at the camera and seeing themselves as serenity for the constantly unsettled in their present. The headscarf wrapped around the head, forming an arc for the contained face and for the stranger's gaze, a headscarf likely made of polyester, of a singular colour. Likely passed on from the mother, or requisitioned from a previous life. The knot is not central, slightly to the right, making the chin more protruding and less veiled. This is my mother looking towards the cameraman, not smiling, in line with the seriousness of the task at hand, and yet, semi-consciously letting go of a look emanating with absentness: I am nowhere to be seen. I am nowhere to be captured entirely.

Then, she was newly married to my father. Then, her first husband would have been dead for a couple of years. I imagine that it was taken while my father was standing in a corner waiting for the cameraman to invite him over to witness the captured and nod in approval. I so want to imagine that it was just fine for her to travel from the camp to the city, carrying her dialect on her back and knowing that, as a refugee, being photographed can be done beyond the question of aid, for the sole reason of being photographed – a fresh topography for a photograph which would leave Baddawi camp in my wallet secretly so as to be archived alongside my moments with my mother, as the son who has always feared her absence to the extent that I, as a child, would hide within the folds of her dress, to accompany her from one camp to another, always in our time and through a no-place which never belonged to us.

I still remember the headscarf or perhaps a headscarf that looked like the one in the photograph, pale like our days. Subdued and modest in colour so as not to project a state of being *contra* the one inside, nor to trick those involved into an existence beyond the means of the existents. The headscarf would have also carried the specks and spectres of the UN rations collected routinely by her. Specks and spectres of flour. Ground and yet with multitudinous weevils that flour was. To remind us of co-existence through the mouth and what it means to see that what we were given was always the unwanted. The cast aside of the perishable as the gift for the cast aside in the refugee. In essence, propitiated with sacrifices that were long dead before reaching us, smothered in their original places to ensure a safe and voiceless delivery for the eternally-grateful needy. My mother would sift the flour through a sieve with holes slightly smaller than the nets attached to all windows shared with the intrusive neighbours. Wall to wall until the camp is no more. My father would regularly fix the sieve, tightening the holes further so no unwanted creatures would reach our bread. Sometimes he would fasten the net around the wooden circle, with little nails. At other times, he would place a new net above the old one, two nets weighing down on what would become our catch of the day.

On the only bed in the house, my father would narrate the same stories. Cross-legged, in a circle we would await his words: stories of better times, of water gushing out of rocks, of long-lost pilgrims watering the desert before their mouths.

It would always be *Once upon a time, there was...* when he began. In that time, his name would be enunciated loud enough, in front of other dusty faces and hungry mouths, to be registered in both Arabic and English as a refugee in the name of a new life in a camp only sprouting in the afterlives of Palestinian times. My father leaning on the wall, arms clasping the void of voids, would grasp what is left of time as though to say: *Be the time that deserts no time, Son. Be my memory for you as much as it is for me.* We would all fall asleep in his bed, the sisters and the brothers, resting on each other's ends.

In time, we would wake up looking for our faces, the faces that my mother would ensure were multiply washed before leaving the house, fresh to study the sciences of what is but never who we are. According to the UN, to learn neutrality in refugee camps where people grow as old as their shadows.

My mother is in front of the camera. Eyes fixated on the barest of movements: one, two, three and the shutter drops one last time - all is done in no time but never dusted. The photograph is taken now, to be processed afterwards. While waiting for the photographs, what did they do to kill yet more time? Did they sit in the only park in the city, arguing about the next time they would accompany one another, talking about their children's insatiable hunger, not knowing where they are? They would collect the photographs in an envelope bearing the name of the photographer but not the photographed. This time they would walk back home to save the taxi fare and retain their silences as they reach the last hill overlooking the camp. The same camp: a sight for the wandering eyes and the blind.

My Mother's Photograph or A Deferred Epitaph

What a scandal scandalises is never the human but the circumstance in which the human is being forced to suspect her humanness. The photograph is also a scandal. It is never an easy task for a refugee whose presence in a hosting state is contingent on her absence to have her photograph taken, in the process being brought to the spotlight as someone to be framed now and in the future. This is my mother's photograph, in black and white, taken for her Identity Card for Palestinian Refugees in Lebanon. The alibi-ID that replaced a life in Palestine with memories with a life in a refugee camp where nothingness awaits itself. To have her photograph taken would have meant that it was time for her ID to be renewed, necessitating newer and fresher photographs of someone who solely ventures outside the camp in an absolute emergency. In this sense, the photograph is not the object itself but a precursor for the ID that is continually passed on in absentia. The photograph would have been countersigned by a stranger at an office outside the camp and clipped at the bottom for it to be stapled like a hanging memory to the new card.

The Crack Invites

There must always be a crack.

In a crack in our old wall, I planted my intentions and left.

Before the same house, in the risen house, narrow and wide at the same time, in the same camp that is, I await your arrival. This time there will be no sacrifices but the dialect. You will borrow mine as we see for the sake of seeing, and I will borrow yours—a dialect for a dialect, noise for noise, to walk the road that is called a camp.

They will slaughter no beast. Nor will they soak their fists with fresh blood to make prints in the newcomer's name. They will say: *It is our blood, whether it is there or not.*

This time they will bear their names on parchments and with the care of unborn things, they will look at you.

I invite you to the limbs of the camp, to an above-place and below-god, to an aridity, infinite, with a name.

I invite you so you would see my mother's swollen feet treading on time as she performs her eternal prayers and despair.

They will stomp on the ground, once, twice, to awaken themselves from this aged dream. There, they will dust their old tools and memories, with hands made of dust, to cook you colours and meat, and wait for another coming.

Hands submitted at the door, draped in shadows and dried coriander. They put forth everything they have, from newborns to sounds, and remind you and themselves: *This is ours since the camp. This is ours since God.*

The crack invites.

The Wait

Hung
                                        or hanged

From a spectral existence to another

For arms   stretched   as far as farness

Suddenness

I wait to see, in my mind's eye, where the crack is.

The Secret

Shhh

I shall tell you a secret

The Arabic *sirr*

My father's bed rocking …

Survival

I
Abide by what is not but shall be one day

II
... or what could be the seen

The criss-crossing on the metal surface

What is meant to endure scratches

The scraps and squabbles of past times

Lending their ears to tomorrow

The Heart is Tomorrow's Absence

What is it that we actually write, if anything, when writing is death attained in writing.

According to them, my body took time to grow. There, there were times when my mother would pray day and night hoping to see me grow into my own body.

Growth in the camp is subject to its time. To keep tabs of who he has seen, the camp's doctor came up with the same name for all dead people.

Whose name is skin
Whose name is superlatively other

To what name shall I return when the war ends?

Forever a fable. The name denigrates those who seek truth in it.

Surviving as one occurs once the heart has replaced the book completely.

Always on his knees, my father would insist on learning by heart. For him, the heart is tomorrow's absence, amassed for another tomorrow.

If appearance is simply returning, absence is definitely the only thing for the future.

And yet what they say in their dialect is what I also say in mine. Always rushed to finish my sentence, I never had time to arrive.

Vows

To Arabic I return
to breathe

in and out

in my heart
shattered urns with the promise to
heal

the once whole
what is now of shards and
dust

a trace still as it is still

english

What is written:
the English I feel in loneliness and pain.

What they once planted for us in borrowed pots

seeds to grow into seedlings

the letters as epitaphs
tombstones for time and its whereabouts

half-immersed in serenity
in cardboard boxes –
all ratified and sellotaped

ready to go

syringes for our not-easily-traceable veins
pills for high blood pressure and other conditions

nothing for the heart

with every initial a word veils
a looming ambush for the fragility in air

craned necks,

homonyms so content in their meanings

Is not English the sudden that remains?

mispronounced in our pronunciation:
a hint of *lugha* or the dialect

to fit our mouths   and
chapped sensibilities

so as to hope to swallow it whole

like pills with dates withheld
from the naked eye,
precise measurements for the imprecise in the ailing body

or to ingest it as instructions dictate
as the complete for the ever-lacking

in living

You benignly call it an accent. I call it a cut.

A scar like the one I was left with   underneath my clothes
deep in the skin

a register – or a parchment?

the repository for every scrap

and the leftovers

Then there was once a tongue that touched –
the spectre in touching.

The voice remembering back:
because my body is devoid of organs I remember it once

In time

I touch within my means – the language that sits to my right the one to my left

like a book that is not yet open

the eye drifting away from *lugha*.

There to exorcise your tongue

Of its intentions.

All that I say, is premised on yours – a stranger to me, a stranger for me.

When I say English, I mean the English in which my sister's veil is never the same.

I say it, the said is said to extricate me from my tongue.

I swear to you, my tongue is tied.

My English should always translate and be translated.

To see the shibboleth, you see the thirsty inevitably
dying en route.

Water offered when death is seen, not for the almost dead.

I no longer see English. What I see is an almost-English perching on my cracked tongue.

Circumcision

They, who were present and took part, decided to move my legs apart. They cut me before allowing me in.

The Bride

He reached that age, or so we were made to believe. My mother was quick to think of those who had faced similar times and too quick to conclude that marrying him off would be the best way to separate him from us and keep our UN rations, as a family, untouched. Nobody had the right to take them away from us, she said. My brother reluctantly accepted. The imam recommended by the uncle had big hands and no vision. He thought for a second then proposed that the cheapest way was for my brother to marry a dead woman on paper whose details could be passed on by another underhand imam.

With everything completed and signatures hastily exchanged we did not celebrate. We sat, imagining a dead woman's face.

Offers

To eat the UN flour
To swallow what comes your way

The nod of the lack,
of what it is that is being gifted;
from tins to thoughts;
from roofs susceptible to fall
to concrete grounds flattened in haste.

The flour equally-halved between us and insects
roaming the place.

To suspect
as you look at what lingers on the plastic mats
where meals and quarrels are had between hungry mouths
that the cooked equates to the edible and
that the things necessarily made
of what is left of the leftovers
are ours in the first place
– the eternal gift.

There, history dictates kissing the hand.
A white, clean hand stretching out from one time to another,
feeding, cutting, wreaking havoc on the imagination
as the pot bubbles over on our makeshift fire
made of everything new and old.
From half-full notebooks
signed with donors' names

to sticks and twigs
collected from all grey corners.
Flour to repel our sight,
as my mother would say.
The dough as a war.
The baked as fire
for the blasphemous.
We sit as norms dictate
munching away
at the scraps
of tomorrow.

Communion

For Anthony Ezekiel (Vahni) Capildeo

We grow nothing. Only the sky.

Lentils.

Because of what they are. What will be of them at the last supper. What we call food so as to remember our bodies fleetingly. What takes time while giving time. Abundant times for us to be hosted by air while straying in differing directions

to distant fates.

Those lentils are not sifted. They are pure and impure. Split and whole. With air and dust we throw them somewhere, a chosen somewhere, a premeditated somewhere, and wait for them to grow as we grow.

Lentils for the mouths that were. The ultimate gift. This is in no way an unconditional gift. Or one given to us in our own hands. But to say that the hands that delivered them to us looked too big. Healthy hands. Hands from a non-camp. Hands that can write names – transliterated names – without hesitation.

Hands that can write imitations of misery with scrupulous detail. Without any fear of going hungry. Without any fear of being struck off the UN register.

Unlike our hands.

The Qur'an's lentils.

Those that feature in the holy books, in our shared mouth.

To steal from the bird's beak, dreams my mother.

The birds that never live in the camp but hover over us in season.

The watery lentils.
The inexhaustible treasures of the poor.
The drowned lentils.
The floating lentils in collective imaginations.

The often talked about of food.   The over-written of bearings.

Why lentils, Anthony?

To eat textually.
To eat the archive.
To eat that which cannot be eaten.
To eat the deluge of tears, long confused with salt.
To eat the exodus in us as companions.
To eat the dreams that could have been truer.
To eat them in the presence of a tongue blocking routes, places and times.
To eat them in order to witness the edible as a witness to us.

My mother who was too young to count and too young for her younger siblings to be left in her care, helplessly bore witness to one of them swallowing uncooked grains and dying.

The parents were ploughing somebody else's fields and scattering their seeds.

My mother still dreams benignly of full stomachs. In her words, *full but not too full*.

Full like our vowels, never bloated.

To this day, she recalls in fragments.

Illicit memories of illicit places.

Like the parting in my sister's hair, is my mother's: what before our eyes is one time. What in our eyes is another. To say: *Both sides are remainders of something and the intended wholeness is a mere scrap for what will touch the cooked*

and later snap.

To make them redder, my mother cooks the lentils with our blood. And if you ask what it is that she does to the pot I would rather not tell you but will whisper it when we next meet.

I will remind you, before food is devoured: The bubbling away of something that returns in some shape or form as something more or less than the original. The crying there is no point to stop. The ending of what is ours in full. As though to say: *Fuck this world for what it will be. Fuck it!* The leftover of the generous.

Hands deeply immersed in the extras, we agree: Eating is not swallowing but touching upon the touched, rendering the moon as fleshy as possible in friendship
and in text.

With your eyes still catching the sight, you stir in all directions. *None is fixed*, you say. None is singular. You stir in your absences and stir in the hope of that created by you – what buds and eventually snaps. What buds again.

The season is the season, secrets hurled in scaled scales for days past.

The War

I am all ears
The bombs I still hear through me

The air raids
Since time

The gravel's flight
From somewhere to nowhere

To what will become of dust

Particles
Those of dissipation

The malevolent
In sounds

The creaking of the door   A gun

The barest of thuds   A raid

A death worthy of its name

Congruence

From the onset,
she places her palms face to face

to bury the void within

For her, shedding tears happens between checkpoints:

a face the shape of sorrow

                wedged between

    her hands   and   silence.

The Razor

I never admitted that I once used his to shave my barely-there beard. What I did not use was a mirror to bear witness to my massacring my face while attempting to shovel blood from one corner to another. My father was a keen shaver and nothing made him more content than a wet shave with an abundance of foam.

I envy your tricks, Father, and wish I understood how, all those years, you managed to master them without cutting yourself.

The Trap

Plough not the voice
Write not the name in suspicion

Your name
As pronounced
    Mispronounced
The trap covered in twigs,
dry leaves and
scraps

to trap the feeble
The wandering soul

      The poet

The good
The evil of letters

Silhouettes of names   making their way to the mouth

Vowed times

Vowels

They call you to witness your coming

The name before you

Dwelling

In the aftermath, he suspects his body remains the same. From the crack of dawn he attends to his existence: from the withered berries with the oats long dry left to their reflection, to the tremor inherited from the father.

No questions to perturb the dryness therein. Nor should he have a reason to suspect that what is before him is his. He is ageing despite everything. Day and night he remembers that age is more than time and the spared time spreading on the empty pages and in every crack is not recitation but time as it is memorised.

From the window, that of the sill and the outside, the season is still counting its clouds, resting on the pronouns of passers-by in anticipation of those long gone.

Holy Water

In the camp, water does not come to us. We summon it from droplets gone astray.
Dragged by mouth until it is before the eye. It is

for those who can draw it out of pipes

chaperone it to their pumps like lost infants forever growing without their mothers.

A helping hand.

A pat on the shoulder.

Many times my father cheated death by chewing it and spitting it out in time's face.
Luring the water that was not, he passed out. Like a snake charmer, summoning the venom in the shape of a creature.

Ailments

His memory is his. His only memory.

The kites we used to fly in the camp's sky were things of beauty, my brother reminded me. He also said that mine never left the ground. Stranded before my feet: a still birth.

Under her pillow were verses that she cannot read.

Her ailments exist in the plural to the extent that no ailment is ever recalled on its own.

We are too many, according to the neighbours. When my mother let go of us, heads on top of heads, our eyes to my mother's utter surprise did not open immediately.

Might what is not the camp, be the camp?

Years have passed since my sister fell and cracked her skull trying to clutch a piece of cucumber thrown to her from the ground to the roof where she was standing. Her injury was so serious, so much so that those who witnessed the fall were able to see through her head.

According to the same sister, strangers' dialects are as discernible as their garments.

Despite the hair, my sister's headscarf also covers the historical wound.

Sinning justifies the body. When we undressed in front of each other, we undressed for us to see our bodies after birth.

To this day, as dictated in norms, the eye that can see is the evil eye.

Whoever sins, knows no language.

Confessions are twisted tongues. The dangling cross in the middle of the room measures recurrence, not the pulse.

Pulses, when fear befalls, remember themselves.

To know where we had been, my father would lick our skin. We once tasted of the sea.

Since we could not afford the barber's, it was either my mother or my older brother who would cut our hair. While attempting to calm my cries, my mother snipped my ear unawares. To this day, my mother says she never did it and that I was born with the mark.

To let go of anger I used to cry myself to sleep.

Reciting over the dead, according to the local imam, is done for the future.

I sometimes wonder what if anything time is for the living.

Air raids awaken speech before the body.

To describe bullet shots as nothing is an understatement uttered to make do with destruction as it comes.

I remember the old woman in the bomb shelter asking us to tread carefully between the dead.

To borrow time, the dead resume thinking in their absence. With the bandage in his hand soaked in fresh blood – the one that fell off his back – he continued to recall how dead he was.

On Living

In the Communist Party Headquarters where my father and eldest brother were members, the only pan, used for frying eggs and cooking, was a piece of metal cut from a box where weapons were once kept.

Then I was too young to come to terms with death and to see death in a light that would be slightly less dim than ours. To toughen me up and expose me to as many dead faces as he could, my brother would drag me along all the funerals he could get hold of. While he was busy chattering, I guardedly unloosened the shroud wrapped over our grandmother's body.

The first time I held a gun was when I decided to shoot time at close range.

After school, or *after after* school, when all visitors had finished with us and the camp, I would ascend to the *jabal* to play with friends. The *jabal* was not a mountain but the arid stretch of land outside the camp where hiding from air raids and the sky was never possible.

There are a few bomb shelters in the camp. Some are requisitioned as houses. Some remain buried under the UNRWA schools. The rest are for the future.

Haram

Haram to leave scraps of bread on the road.
(Put them aside for insects and birds)

Haram to turn your back on food – the same food cooked over and over again.
(Eat it gratefully)

Haram to steal from people's rations.
(Steal from shops)

Haram to look at your naked mother.
(Look at her wound)

Haram to desert a refugee camp.
(Carry it with you)

Haram to forge your father's signature.
(Tell them he is dead)

Haram to dwell on time.
(Kill it at once)

Haram to mourn excessively.
(Cry in anticipation)

Haram not to surrender your morbid thoughts.
(Lie to the imagination)

Haram not to be breastfed for two terms.
(Sense the ending)

Haram to see all things.
(Eyes for the temporary)

Haram to write over writing.
(Bodies are bare)

Haram not to hear the bombing.
(I hear it in one ear)

Haram to hunt down metonymies.
(Drag them from the heart)

Haram to see the body stark naked.
(Bodies are martyrs)

Haram not to ponder with every breath.
(Forsaken patience)

Haram to cut trees and desecrate forests.
(Suspended coffins)

Haram to stare at faces – and look and look.
(See not a human)

Haram to kiss while quenched.
(Expansive lands are lips)

Haram to want what you do not have.
(Sustenance is for tomorrow)

Haram to envy the dead.
(Envy the anonymous in dying)

Haram not to return home.
(My mother's cane is long forlorn)

Haram to shave in front of your father.
(Poetry and hair are ostensibly the same)

Haram to be occupied by vowels.
(Letters of ailment leave my soul)

Haram to borrow the neighbour's barrow.
(The bearer is another doubt)

Haram not to love the ill.
(*Alif* is sane and sound)

Haram to translate the name.
(Ninety-nine belong to God)

Haram to hold your breath.
(Air is a language)

Haram to promise a name before birth.
(A stray bullet pronounces the dead)

Haram to implore the United Nations in spite of God.
(Food perishes in the mouth)

Haram to dislike your sister's poetry.
(Hate her husband)

Haram not to attend to the missing plants in your imagination.
(Water the ungraspable)

Haram to fight over the scarce.
(Fragility is a second coming)

Haram to remember for your parents.
(Senility shall come)

Haram to write for your mother.
(Write her)

The Name

I
From the *raised*

traded for an otherwise presence,

to spirits

gathering to dislodge the body,

ruffling its limbs.

The *anonymous*

always on guard.

II
I could swear that my name lies in memory.

III
My claiming asylum happened on unclaimed territories.

IV
I was constantly reminded that for the claim to make sense, I needed to reclaim the name.

V
In their eyes, when a name is handed over, it is to be verified as a name for the yet-to-be-named.

VI

It is in the name that I am pronounced alive and dead at the same time.

VII

When they first asked for my name, I dissected the sounds with a scalpel so the name's innards became too bare not to be seen.

VIII

Once the name is misspelt, attending to the fault-line becomes a matter of time.

My name – is it not the anti-body taking the body's hand?

When the Officer asked again for my name, I could not but laugh.

Since when are names inanimate?

When I was left to fend for myself on the streets of Manchester I hid in my name.

IX

The Name
> *A tombstone*
> *A reclusive shadow*
> *A relic*
> *An amulet for the evil eye*
> *A deciduous memory*

X

No one can survive a misspelt name.

XI

My mother, to remember how old she is, remembers the catastrophe.

XII

Since misspelling happens only once, the name dies then.

Why is it that it is the one name that is misspelt?

A refugee's name is evidence to survival.

Can you not see that a misspelt name is a wounded name?

A Gate Cut Out of Dreams
Dear Officer

Forever grateful I will be
to the line you retraced across my fragile *name*

through the *date of birth*

all the way to my *heart*

cross-examining my intentions

no *eye-contact*

                               or welcoming poetics to tame the
abnormal in the air

palms resting on overcrowded texts

a nib-less pen to the side to gesture for the path that wasn't

a line from a past interview for me to follow–

a fault-line

I stand before you

a leather briefcase   freshly tagged for the occasion

nothing of significance inside

barely a few documents to remember who I am

Handed over so you could see the other inscribed in yesterday's ink

My hand opening   shutting

                                              letting go

and

Recoiling

I whisper to the air between us: Those are the tremors that remain the involuntary dancing for a deferred promise

the body curdling its body

whose difference is no longer different but a patterned mould for the same

for the refugee after

for the refugee before

for the face to become a trap

A borne scandal –

for the hastening crowds to cast a glance

The projection of my voice   from a safe distance   to the guttural thoughts in my head

Gait, for you, to measure the body in motion

To standardise the pain of fleeing
of bodies falling into one

For me, *the gate* that is slammed shut in my face

A thwarted escape from place to place

A gate cut out of dreams

Of what will never be

so on and so forth

I wait at the threshold

It is time to remember that in the shade of waiting, seeing grows

I walked to come to you in my other's absence

on earth

the my as difference

as an attached pronoun steadying a tilting frame

I know that what I say is a minor detail in your eyes

My broken veins, a damaged inside

Signs of a former life

Wreathed in Vowels

I return to my mother tongue – the tongue of an illiterate mother.

[But is the return not an admission of a desertion in the first place?]

To reattach myself to sounds as sparse as a line of ants, hoping that my remembering who I am enables me to translate myself into language.

a stranger   *Wreathed in vowels*

a stranger   *A circumcised tongue*

For it is a Calf

> A cognate of *lugha* (language), *laghā* is the calf that does not count towards indemnity or blood money due to its insignificant stature and vulnerable age —Abū Manṣūr Al-Azharī, 895-980 AD

I
Lugha
a tongue it is.

Many,
Forked

Tongues.

An equivalence to life in death

                              To Man and beast

II
I speak in tongues.

Groans of cast-off calves

too feeble to count
too frail to tip the scale.

III
The calf is language.

In traditions, a needless birth since its name.

A never-lived age   or just a living – that of the lack in life

When killings are customarily settled

Over unmourned carcasses.

English

I

Who should we ask before writing in English? The language we see in ellipses. Symbols, for us, for survival as relics in the camps, where those with pulses like ours could sense. The premeditated language from them to us, on everything that we do not own: ration cards, pills, textbooks, roofs, tins, sacks of rice, flour and cracked wheat, powdered milk, ghee, distribution centres, schools and clinics. The new-borns, rummaging from breast to breast, hanging from swings and donations, other, more voiced, cries to shoulder their cries so the UN would become a text for the foreseeable in living. The shibboleth so we pass. To walk in lines, in preassigned places, where hostility and hospitality are mere synonyms. This is not history but its afterlife. No one to question our dying. No one to shed a tear for what is happening behind walls. Thin, flawed walls built for the temporary in mind. To once again attend to the inners of language. Like our private parts smothered with talcum powder and later sins, wrapped in diapers bearing logos in English, capital letters, so bodies are ratified as they grow out of life, as they succumb to the same hands and manuals. Bodies measured according to weight and waiting...

II

From a mother to her son: Language? Deficiency incarnate. The confined animal raised on the bare minimum of grass to gain weight and sound for the imminent slaying.

The Body

I hold it in my right
the blameless revelation beneath the skin

The notebook he once scribbled in
the past poems for a torn time

Page after page, the signed that was his
rhymes – incomplete – amassed for the ill heart

I remember him pouring water on us
to grow like distant trees

The glasses fogging up until there was no sight
the scrubbed bodies cast aside and the ones waiting in the background

Until came the time, men and women in separate lines muttering words
the sons in the yard washing the dead father

Home is a Tomb

A cut separating the flesh from the flesh.

When bombs fall, people hear themselves.

My mother would shout with every bang to cover our ears thinking that this would be sufficient not to hear.

The shattered body was that of a young man who was trying to see where the bomb was heading.

Solemnity that is the word that weighs the most and sinks with the heart.

Over wine and other things, she asked me to describe the camp. There was a wide sea between us and enough food to feed the entire nation, and people coming and going without any noise.

To describe is to circumcise the past.

The Arabic verb *describe* loses a limb on its way to imminence.

From memory comes the last breath.

Foreigners set in the west and rise in the east.

Those shouldering a coffin always comment on the weight of the borne.

The lighter the better – this is what the bearded man said on the way to bury my father.

The silent sound in *bayt* (home) and *qabr* (tomb) is always in the middle.

For the mourners:

Home is the tomb.

The greener the plants, the more death there will be.

The refugee camp is difference engendering itself. For the life of me, I cannot remember the last time I have not thought of the camp.

As my mother cuts my hair, she trims the loose plots I grew in my heart.

Opacity – my tongue speaks in tongues - *After Glissant*

Articulating pain happens in the body. My father would embrace me so I would not go.

How many times did I tell my father that I loved him? Not a single time. My love for him was non-verbal and as tense as silence.

Read me out loud so I renounce your voice in me.

In the divine I set foot in my dreams.

My mother had two cloths: one for her periods, the other to drain water out of yogurt.

I remember traces of blood on the clothesline drying in the sun.

I once cut it to draw blood. Copious amounts running through my arm. For a while, I mistrusted myself not dying.

Europe – I came to you   not wanting to come

To historicise is to see your image reflected in void.
A view culminates in breathing.

What cuts through words is also breathing.

My therapist, to use it as an opportunity to tie his shoelaces, would recount how overwatered climbers defy the point of watering.

Water cheats death.

To live is to live within a chain

The stretch from life to living on the way to living on

Like treading on earth   a face's turn to see

A siege – if you wish

That is to move from place to place without moving, or

Survive to live life beyond its means

Think of glass

(a name with a receding hairline)

Shattered

for it to be called a past to the thing that was

But this shattering is also *darning*

to rejoin the once whole to call it an eye

Letters of Ailment

Letters of ailment
Sounds of the obscure
Waterless gargling
Like wells, suspicious of their void
Fortune-tellers untying spells
Untying times

(Spells for time)

With every vowel a stranger's tongue is severed
To tell who it is that is an other
In Arabic, the superlative other

Who it is whose self is that of doubt

(Doubts are languages)

Languages with knuckles
Languages with spleens

I translate my tongue, the leftover as ash to ash. As suspicions for myself. For the trembling in me and language. Signs, deprived of laps, planted in all times. Seasons reminiscent of themselves – long and ponderous. You and me, host and guest, swapping limbs and languages – remembering each other's names in each other's bodies

(Bodies in sight)

The Story

Because my name is the story
Of what it is that is named
Because I am the named

His active voice   masculine

The passive   the disappeared

From the   Name
The named is unnamed

Coupled with distance

Draped in unfamiliar sounds

I knock

Knock Knock Knock

To render the sound a cut
Not to forget   it is the English language
In the sound
In the written

In the throat

I knock

Splendid wood, filled-in cracks so it looks as new as its past,
Smooth
Multiply-treated
Of all befallen illnesses

Sacred wood

The cross

Uprooted lives

The beating to awake

I knock

Knock Knock Knock

Soft, subtle – perhaps too subtle,
whispered bangs   so not to
Disorder the time you're in
The trance
from the threshold to the innards of the place
Etcetera etcetera

Where cloaks
And times are suspended in order

Spectres for the impending bodies?

The exact same bodies
The white bodies
The bodies incarnated in bodies

Soft, subtle – perhaps too subtle,
whispered bangs   so not to
disturb the breath that is breathed in
and out
the wardrobe
the mahogany extras

The religiously-cleaned mirror
Room for reflection
To see the self naked
in deferred confessions

The art in the artifice

The line of argumentation
Way before the seen
The scene from your room as usual:
Old trees
Old plants
Once stuffed birds
And eyes
The skin you hold dear
The legs shaking to shake
Those with fear
Those with never-strong-hearts

I say in whispers
In Oxford,
in the city that is Greater than god,
I know
I know my knowledge
Through the text
And the body – my body
The hair the bones
The flesh there and here

Through the mother

Umm

In the Qur'an thrice as present as the father

The noun – and name
Taken by hand to the pronoun – the conscience therein

A trembling hand

In the language I speak

[Through the reading of my palm:
There is God for her.
There is the Prophet.
And because my heart is inside hers
I will know her knowledge by heart].

But you made me stutter in your English
To mind sentences about camps, refugees
And

The things I read in depression
For depression

Theory   the flesh
Theory   the bones
Theory   God

To render the sound a cut

Because my name is the story
Of what it is that is named
Because I am the named

To Wait is to See

From the beginning, we were asked to wait. Expected to summon time over and wait, and be grateful for what comes our way, from anywhere. Or what runs away beyond our sight. To wait for God appearing bare. For his eventual intervention and the heavens he scaffolds for various conditions and states. To wait for those who reach us through the moans. Who suspect that because of hunger people growl; they become beasts, ciphers, ferocious and benevolent at once. They are here to help. To rescue us from our selves and to teach us what it is that should be sought for day and night. To be visited by those we call guests, by those freckled and white ghosts who enter and exit us with the barest of sounds.

I remember spotting them from their height, their healthy tummies. Not too bloated. Not too concave. Full tummies covered in handsome clothes. Cologned bodies, unlike ours. Always resonant. Always present despite our absence. We would get up for them. Sweep the roads. Decorate our temporary walls and sit silently awaiting their sacred statures.

We wait to see. This is precisely what we were taught in our language. Waiting is seeing. Cognates of the same site and time. A root for rootless memories. Never in the dialect but in the purest of registers. To wait is to see. Seeing as a contraction for waiting. A contraction giving birth to bigger, anticipating eyes. A birth. A wound. The eyes to see while all waits.

Abolition

He who never sets foot in   the camp
calls for the abolition of the camp

He prophesies

A prophet he is
bearing a book in his right
for the vanished
the colonised

A rendition for the heart to lose its body,
the refugee to die elsewhere,
and if dead to die more

The one who is   not ever sad-drunk,
Never placeless in dreams,

remembered not in excess

thinks that sorrow is sufficient to kill my mother's god,
to set Her rug on fire

An effigy it is not

A stretch of land
leading to god

He prophesies

to make history begin elsewhere
so living can be ordained by hands

The hands of one body
Resurrected in words
Stroked so they wince at time

What happens to us, happens to our dead

For it is Death
That does more than the living

In digging a grave or severing a shadow

When hands touch and are touched by earth

In memory lies tomorrow

In tombs frequented with empty hands
In tears still warm
They remain warm

The camp never perishes.

Verses repeated at length
In a clear loud voice
To repel the excess in Death

To countersign the ever-escaping in speech

To draw a circle for eyes not to flee
$$\text{but dwell}$$

To circumscribe the seen by blindfolding the unseen

Us as the object

The enigma in life

Sacrilege in abundance

He prophesies to resurrect the dead

I say in the hope of not saying
What I cannot but say
For the old, the young and
The in-between
As though to say:
I was in a no-place
where living is measured by the now

Not by what came its way once

When the past can also be a mother –

A path

To spectral shadows –

Their time

To gifts surrendered at the doorstep

To ether

Whose people have long left their sites to
Make up for missed prayers

As though the camp were one

As though the camp were contagious

Ill for you
Ill for us

We wait

Slain Intentions

It takes as long as it takes to remember what memory is: on tenterhooks, sometimes in someone else's language. Or stored away in wooden boxes. Sometimes spotted in piles of expired dates. This is when fingers palpate the edges of something that is neither seen nor unseen but does not mind a stranger's touch. I remember the day my father made us hold his gun, each in turn, before handing it over to his comrade for the last time. It was an AK47 with a wooden butt, engravings from a previous life, a barely visible heart, asymmetrical, likely drawn by a young fighter, by a wishful lover, with an arrow permeating through, with a faint name on one end and a question mark on the other.

At my old school as a dare we would be asked whether we had ever seen a dead person. Always excluding family members.

To kill time we would normally disappear for hours without our parents' consent to places where dissident lovers meet, where leftovers of bodies and things are cast aside, to collect fossils and scrap metal to later sell or barter for more fossils and some food.

Is the camp not an archaeological site – countless sites collapsing into one space that since time has been living on a drip.

Grotesque is what it is.
Ash for the eyes.
Ash for the dying that is never content.

The one who thinks that the camp is finished when it is written always forgets what my name is.

When my father named me despite my mother he named me for my own sake.

I stand alone. Holding the scraps of language in one hand and begging for water in the other.

To speak another language, to be recited upon in another.

When God asks in language, He asks to scourge the sound that is not.

To this day, I dare my sister to remember what it felt like when the bomb fell near her.

Inside the bomb shelter, the one closest to our house, lays a mattressless metal bed. One which was never lifted out of the shelter. Nor was it claimed by anyone. It was, as my father would vouch in every conversation, the one used to elevate the dead from the living so we as kids would not digress.

The woman who would ask my brother to pick some figs off her tree never liked me. In her eyes, the figs I had once picked were not ripe enough.

Or I could not feel ripeness
In my hands

Snatching
Not intently touching for it to count

Fig after fig, paraded before our eyes,
on a piece of cloth,

Spotty,
Spotted – then

so she palpated the flesh underneath
so she claimed the tree in meaning

*The touch a means
to the mouth,*

The forever hungry mouth

*Castoffs:
First twisted
Not in order*

*Today inedible
memorialised in urns and glass*

*Whatever the ripe is
It is life anticipating its end*

Ketchup! Ketchup!

Mother, make us that that you are yet to see.

Giving in to our requests to consume what was seen during that time as the unknown, my mother accepted to make us some ketchup from our rations. It was her unusual reading that a simple tin of tomato paste from the UN, normally added to another UN staple, cracked wheat, to make it more palatable and less pale, did not only have the material ingredients to create a new substance, but was also the very focal point for what was considered otherworldly at that time. Her aim as conveyed while deep at work was to create the new out of the rationed – and the already limited. My mother had never seen that ketchup nor had she tasted it, but through our taste buds and constant raving about this new thing she opted for a similar colour.

By not believing that ketchup is entirely present in its own form, my mother rejected the blind acceptance of the new as new, as she attempted to recreate the same. Her desire to promote, in her eyes, the unnoticeable difference between a bottle of ketchup that she

had never seen and a tin of tomato paste almost made her actions believable. Translating the process into a creation of sorts, she reinscribed the value of colour: a movement from red to another shade of red through a rereading of what was deemed as the real red in the first place. After hours attempting to produce ketchup, she gave up, without acknowledging that her trials were a waste of time and our tomato paste, and to a certain extent an unintentional dilution of something that we decided not to remember well.

In our little eyes, punctuated with the rationed red, unaccustomed as they were to too many colours, but to our red, my mother owned our take on the unknown, submitting what she had never seen or tasted, before our eyes, so we would see with her.

Prayers II

What comes of clouds
    Of their constant returns and
                       Departures
The murky life underneath the splintered nail
The mud attributed to growing

Growing up

like no other growth

What comes of them

Those times moving by not moving
The unexpected knots – within –
harbouring doubts

Doubts about everything that moves
That stagnates

About the living
Living up high
Either with Him or in his well-rummaged House

What comes of them
the djinns   the angels

The Devil crowing over
Sins

His wish for severed intentions and

blood

Sins at arm's length   still in the heart

The Ration Card

I
What does it mean

for existence to be certified by a piece of paper

bearing a unique number

a translated name from Arabic to English   a date of birth

a place in folds:

memories from there

more memories budding in refugee camps

Now laminated, safeguarded, computerised

Smart-looking

Continue to *cause sharp pain*

Binding pains,

some inherited

Some not

Before hand-written by someone who we might even know

the father of a father?

the mother of a mother?

II
Inscribed

Reinscribed in English

The inimitable English

The *transliteration* as more-than-a-name

As the name despite our names

Recorded in haste like our Exodus

Carried through until death

Without this text no presence to see

an absent presence

nipped in the bud

A Decent Burial

The worst of deaths is that which does not recognise dying as whole. Without any remorse, we killed the grasshoppers. The killing was a fact. But to this day, I am still at a loss to why we arranged their little dismembered bodies on a piece of paper before offering them, in our eyes, a decent burial.

The Cull

Amongst the invalid bodies amassed by the yellow trees, there was a fawn, a single one, moaning at the end of its outing.

Holes

I
How will I die
While all
Can see me?

II
I was born
On the seam of a dress,
In the last hour
Of the sixth day,
Between clusters of stars
And the borders of a river.

I was neither
Adam reaching the ground,
Nor was I myself
In cities
Which share their water
With the agents of doom.

III
I lean on
The footsteps of my past
As I slip towards
My shadow.

The shadow which I left
Lying
Outside our house
On the morning
Of that funeral.

I am that dead person
But I don't know
How
He managed to escape.

IV
Upside down
And in the middle
Of the yard
His picture was hung.
They did not change
The place of the pail.
He will cry,
And the image
Will float on the
Face of the pail.

Family Album

I

Then, to wash meant to carry everything to the river
To immolate at its bank
The river the camp holds as a companion from a distance
Eternally stretched arms

Nahr Al-Bared, its name:

> *Nahr*   river
> *Bared*   cold
> *Al*   the definite article tucked in between

What travelled in a stranger's sack to another land

Could the definite not come

Not make it to the heart

Delay its arrival a while

> So what is named is named prior to time

The camp would arrive later

Where the other part of the family lived

Aunts, young, uncovered, at the river,
my mother at its bank, then a girl, with fair plaits
scrubbing pots and garments
So together they save time for the days to come
So together, after counting themselves many times, they enter the camp
While they dig in other people's fields
They talk to themselves, monologues coming and going,
Hushed when it is day

Heard at night:

Better to dig in other people's fields than not to dig
Our land belongs to God
Our beasts slain for heavens in our absence

II
He would peek to see their flesh afresh and dream of the days things and bodies were bare. My aunt, the middle one, was lurking behind the reeds as the rest were ravaging the water with God knows what. With the dress wrapped around her waist, and a rolling pin in one hand, one, two bangs, and he fell into the river, blood seeping into their things.

III
She was made a second wife. That was my grandmother's wish to marry her off to the first man to knock on their door. He was as old as my grandfather, not as ill, but never as kind. People would ask her to wait, things one day would change. My mother, instead, handed her some rat poison and said: *Get rid of that piece of shit. Get rid of him now.*

IV
To come to terms with pain I set my mother's dress on fire to put it out with my own bare hands.

V
Grab it by the neck! Grab it until it changes colour. From where I sat, I could see the bruised neck but not the man. He was nowhere to be seen.

VI
Unlike its bearer, the mouth wanders on the edge of things.

Acknowledgements

I am grateful to the editors of the following magazines, journals, and books, where a number of poems included in this collection were originally published in their current or earlier versions: *New England Review*, *Migrant Knowledge*, *Migration and Society*, *Modern Poetry in Translation*, *PN Review* and *Poetry London*.

The following poems were commissioned by and/or formed part of my work with a number of initiatives: 'The Name' and 'A Gate Cut out of Dreams' were commissioned by the Institute of Statelessness and Inclusion; 'UNRWA,' 'The Divination Bowl,' 'Other Remains,' 'Communion,' 'The War', 'On Living,' 'The Body,' 'The Ration Card' and 'Family Album' were undertaken as part of my work as co-lead of the Baddawi Camp Lab as part of the Imagining Futures AHRC Network Plus programme; 'Writing with my Mother,' 'The Crack Invites' and 'Offers' were written during my work as Writer in Residence of the AHRC-ESRC Refugee Hosts research project; and 'A Photograph for my Mother's Absence' and 'A Swelling in Time' were composed in conversation with the ERC Crossroads of Knowledge research project.

My most heartfelt thanks and appreciation to the Society of Authors for awarding me an Authors' Foundation grant to support my writing.

In gratitude to those who have read and critically engaged with my writing over the years, supporting and commenting on my work from near and afar: Serena Alagappan, Seth Anziska, Charlie Baylis, Mette L. Berg, Elleke Boehmer, James Byrne, Anthony Ezekiel (Vahni) Capildeo, Amal de Chickera, Natalya Din-Kariuki, Elena Fiddian-Qasmiyeh, Catherine Gander, Mina Gorji, Marilyn Hacker, Séan Hewitt, Elena Isayev, Chloé Lewis, John McAuliffe,

Jamie McKendrick, Andrew McMillan, Stuart McPherson, Jessica Mookherjee, Kim Moore, Laura Morowitz, Subha Mukherjee, André Naffis-Sahely, Jeremy Noel-Tod, Bernard O'Donoghue, Karl O'Hanlon, Mohamed-Salah Omri, David Owen, Mariangela Palladino, Sandeep Parmar, Tom Paulin, Eleanor Paynter, Matthew Reynolds, Anna Roper Rowlands, Philippe Sands, Tristam Fane Saunders, Lyndsey Stonebridge, Shash Trevett, Pádraig Ó Tuama, Katica Urbanc, and Rowan Williams.

Finally, I am hugely indebted to Aaron Kent and *Broken Sleep Books* for their continuous support and for believing in my work.

This book is for Bissan-Maria Fiddian-Qasmiyeh, Elena Fiddian-Qasmiyeh and my family in Baddawi camp and beyond.

LAY OUT YOUR UNREST

www.ingramcontent.com/pod-product-compliance
Lightning Source LLC
LaVergne TN
LVHW041259080426
835510LV00009B/807